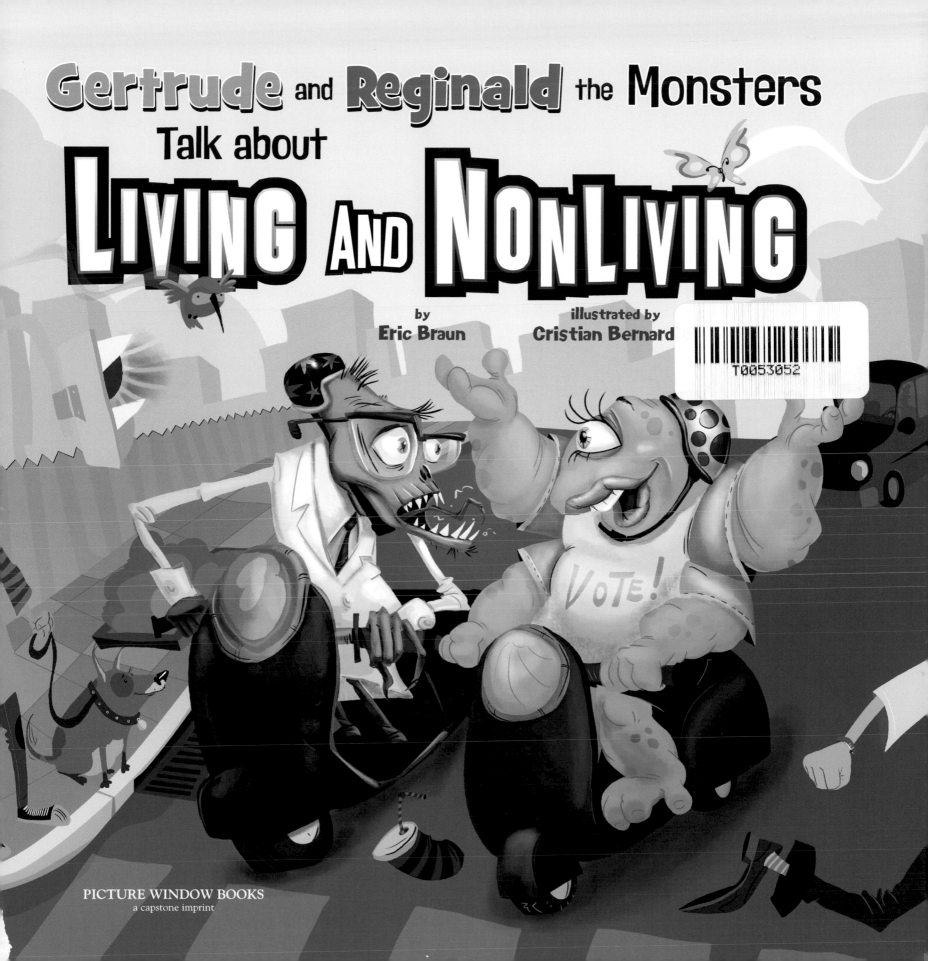

Gertrude and Reginald the Monsters Talk about LIVING AND NONLIVING

by Eric Braun

illustrated by Cristian Bernard

T0053052

PICTURE WINDOW BOOKS
a capstone imprint

Thanks to our advisers for their expertise, research, and advice:
Dr. Paul Ohmann, Associate Professor of Physics, University of St. Thomas
Terry Flaherty, PhD, Professor of English, Minnesota State University, Mankato

Editor: **Gillia Olson**
Designer: **Lori Bye**
Art Director: **Nathan Gassman**
Production Specialist: **Danielle Ceminsky**
The illustrations in this book were created digitally.

Picture Window Books
1710 Roe Crest Drive
North Mankato, MN 56003
www.capstonepub.com

Library of Congress Cataloging-in-Publication Data
Braun, Eric, 1971–
  Gertrude and Reginald the monsters talk about living and nonliving /
written by Eric Braun ; illustrated by Cristian Bernardini.
    p. cm. — (In the science lab)
  Includes bibliographical references and index.
  ISBN 978-1-4048-7146-5 (library binding)
  ISBN 978-1-4048-7237-0 (paperback)
  1. Life (Biology)—Juvenile literature. 2. Organisms—Juvenile
literature. 3. Biology—Juvenile literature. I. Bernardini, Cristian,
1975– ill. II. Title. III. Title: Living and nonliving.
  QH501.B73 2012
  570—dc23   2011029684

Gertrude and Reginald are friends, but they don't always agree. For example, Gertrude prefers funny books, while Reginald likes serious ones. Gertrude loves candy corn smoothies. Reginald is into salad.

THEY ARE BOTH MONSTERS, BUT REGINALD DOESN'T LIKE THAT WORD.

"IT'S RUDE!" HE SAYS.

"But Reggie," said Gertrude.

"YOU HIDE UNDER BEDS AND SCARE PEOPLE, JUST LIKE ME. YOU AND I ARE THE SAME."

Reginald looked down his nose at his friend.

SHE WAS SLIMY, SMELLY, AND HAPPY. "I AM NOTHING LIKE YOU," HE SAID.

Gertrude rubbed one of her chins. She hated to argue. But she didn't want Reginald to go through life thinking he was so different.

"ACTUALLY, YOU AND I ARE BOTH LIVING THINGS. THAT MEANS WE HAVE TONS IN COMMON."

"Ha!" said Reginald.
"Like what?" he asked, as if he really wanted to know.

5

Gertrude said, "You eat, don't you? All living things have to eat. They need water too."

Reginald watched Gertrude make yet another candy corn smoothie. Yuck, he thought. But he had to admit, they both needed to eat.

"But plants are alive," he said. "And they don't eat."

"Plants make their own food by using light," said Gertrude. "Their eating doesn't look like our eating. But it's really the same."

Gertrude continued, "You and I use food to make energy, just like all living things. We use that energy to do things we need to do, like move around. We can notice things around us, and we can react to them. Like if it's cold, we can put on a jacket. If there's danger, we can run away. Things that aren't alive can't do that stuff."

"Are you telling me that plants can move?" asked Reginald.

"Actually, yes," replied Gertrude. "Plants grow and bend toward the light. Sunflowers will turn to face the sun as it moves across the sky."

Reginald raised his eyebrows. "That's quite amazing," he said.

Gertrude paused. She was going to talk about something Reginald would think is disgusting.

She said, "ALL LIVING THINGS GET RID OF WASTE."

"YOU MEAN LIKE TAKE OUT THE TRASH?" Reginald laughed. "YOU NEVER DO THAT!"

"NO," Gertrude giggled. "I MEAN GO POOP."

"Oh," said Reginald. "I know you do that, because it smells!"

"You do it too, Reggie," she reminded him.

Reginald blushed.

Reginald had an idea. "So living things eat, use energy, and poop ... um, get rid of waste. Right?"

"Right."

"So what about your scooter? It gets energy from gas—that's its food. It uses the energy to motor around. And using the gas makes exhaust. That's waste. Are you going to tell me your scooter is alive?"

REGINALD SMILED. HE HAD CAUGHT GERTRUDE THIS TIME!

"Of course not," said Gertrude. "Living things can reproduce. A scooter can't do that."

"Reproduce?" asked Reginald.

"Make more of itself. Animals, like people and monsters, make babies. Plants, like banana trees and grass, make seeds that can grow into new plants. Some tiny living things like bacteria just divide in two."

Reginald crossed his arms. Smarty-pants Gertrude had an answer for everything! "We're not allowed to scooter until our work is done," he huffed.

14

15

"My work is done. Don't change the subject," Gertrude said.

"Well, rules are important, that's all," said Reginald.

"True," said Gertrude. "Here's a rule:

ALL LIVING THINGS BREATHE.

You breathe. I breathe. We all breathe."

"Plants don't breathe!" said Reginald. "Bacteria don't breathe!"

"They do," replied Gertrude.

"They sure do, Reggie."

"That's crazy talk!" Reginald said.

"Plant and bacteria breathing is different from our breathing, but they use air to release energy. Same as us."

DON'T

DON'T

DON'T

DO

Gertrude said, "Every living thing is the same in those ways. If something does not do one of those things, then it is not living.

NONLIVING THINGS MIGHT BE A PART OF THE NATURAL WORLD, LIKE WATER AND ROCKS."

"Or they can be made by living things, right?" Reginald asked. "Like scooters are made by people."

"That's right, Reggie," said Gertrude.

"THERE IS SOME BAD NEWS," Gertrude said.
"ALL LIVING THINGS DIE SOMEDAY."

"Oh," said Reginald. "That is bad news."

"I'm still glad to be a living thing," Gertrude said. "We get to be friends while we're alive. And we get to do fun things like ride scooters together. That's pretty unique, don't you think?"

"I GUESS IT IS," Reginald agreed.

"Hey Gertrude, how did you get to be so smart?" asked Reginald.

"It's just the way I am, I guess." Gertrude thought for a moment. "Actually, you're pretty smart, too, you know. That's another way you and I are alike."

"YOU'RE A GOOD FRIEND, GERTRUDE. I'M GLAD WE'RE SO ALIKE."

Glossary

bacteria—tiny living things that live all around us and inside us

energy—the power that living things use to do all the tasks needed to live

exhaust—the waste gases made by a motor

reproduce—when living things make more of themselves

waste—what a living thing does not use after food or other nutrients have been digested

To Learn More

More Books to Read

Bang, Molly, and Penny Chisholm. *Living Sunlight: How Plants Bring the Earth to Life.* New York: Blue Sky Press, 2009.

Kalman, Bobbie. *Is It a Living Thing?* Introducing Living Things. New York: Crabtree Pub. Co., 2008.

Rau, Dana Meachen. *Life.* Earth Matters. New York: Marshall Cavendish Benchmark, 2009.

Rissman, Rebecca. *Is It Living or Nonliving?* Chicago: Heinemann Library, 2009.

Internet Sites

FactHound offers a safe, fun way to find Internet sites related to this book. All of the sites on FactHound have been researched by our staff.

Here's all you do:

Visit *www.facthound.com*

Type in this code: 9781404871465

Super-cool stuff! Check out projects, games and lots more at **www.capstonekids.com**

InDEx

LOOK FOR ALL THE BOOKS IN THE SERIES:

CAPTAIN KIDD'S CREW
EXPERIMENTS WITH

SINKING AND FLOATING

DO-4U THE ROBOT
EXPERIENCES

FORCES AND MOTION

Gertrude and Reginald the Monsters
Talk about

LIVING AND NONLIVING

JOE-JOE THE WIZARD BREWS UP

SOLIDS, LIQUIDS, AND GASES